Favorite Hy
for Solo Guitar

T0045654

Arranged by Marcel Robinson

ISBN 978-0-634-02798-7

HAL•LEONARD®
CORPORATION
7777 W. BLUEMOUND RD. P.O. BOX 13819 MILWAUKEE, WI 53213

Visit Hal Leonard Online at
www.halleonard.com

Abide With Me

Words by Henry F. Lyte
Music by William H. Monk

Intro
Moderately slow

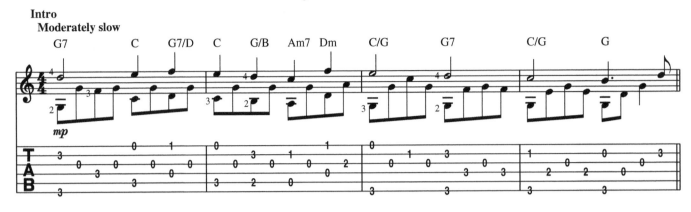

Verse

1. A - bide with me. Fast falls the e - ven
2. I need Thy pre - sence ev - 'ry pass - ing

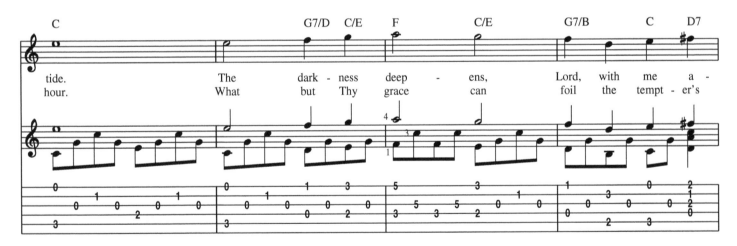

tide. The dark - ness deep - ens, Lord, with me a -
hour. What but Thy grace can foil the tempt - er's

bide. When oth - er help - ers
pow'r? Who, like Thy - self, my

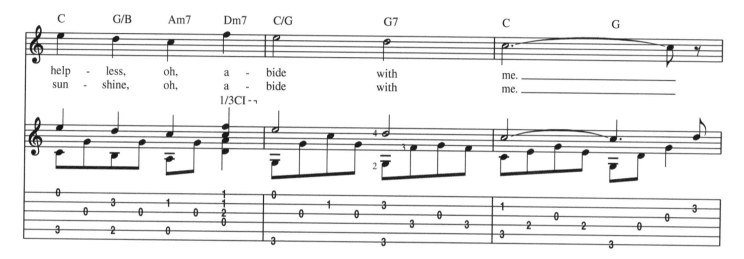

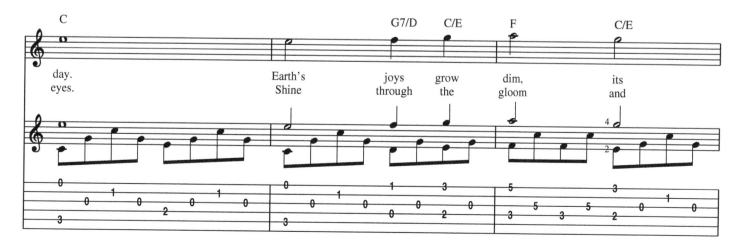

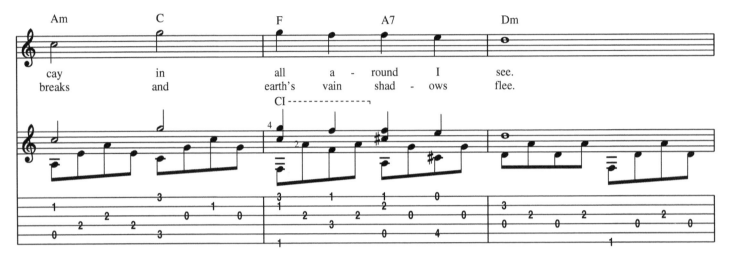

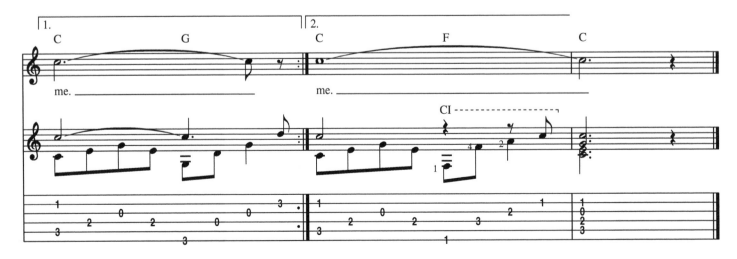

Amazing Grace

Words by John Newton
From A Collection of Sacred Ballads
Traditional American Melody
From Carrell and Clayton's Virginia Harmony
Arranged by Edwin O. Excell

Drop D tuning:
(low to high) D - A - D - G - B - E

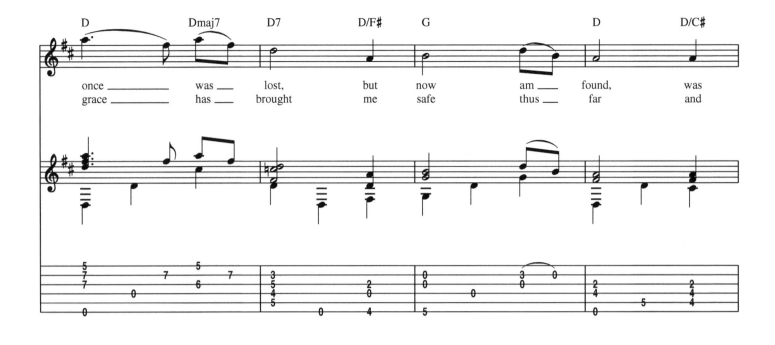

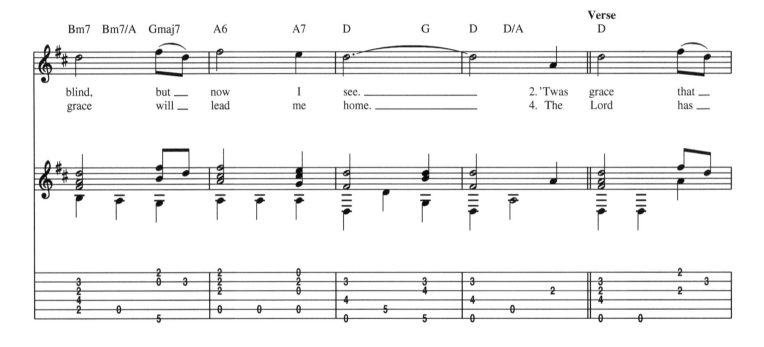

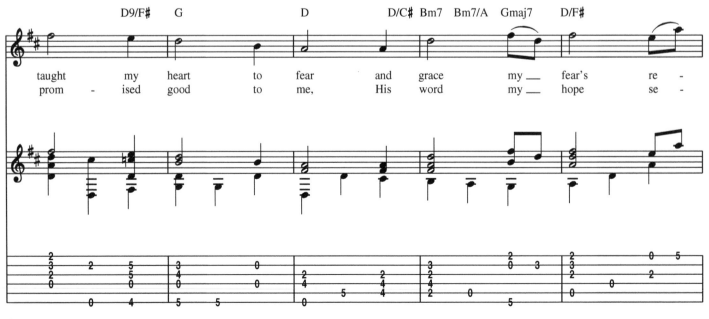

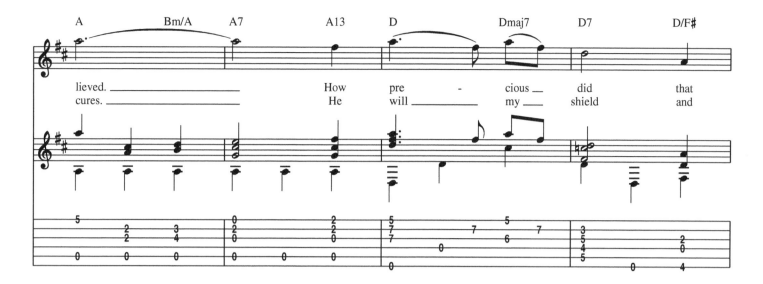

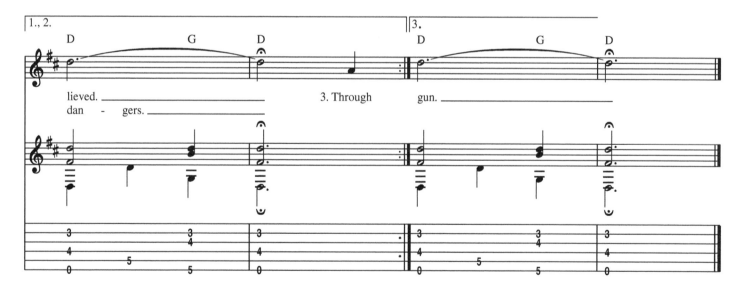

Additional Lyrics

5. And when this flesh and heart shall fail
   And mortal life shall cease.
   I shall possess within the veil
   A life of joy and peace.

6. When we've been there ten thousand years,
   Bright, shining as the sun.
   We've no less days to sing God's praise
   Than when we first begun.

Be Thou My Vision

Traditional Irish

Translated by Mary E. Byrne

Drop D tuning:
(low to high) D - A - D - G - B - E

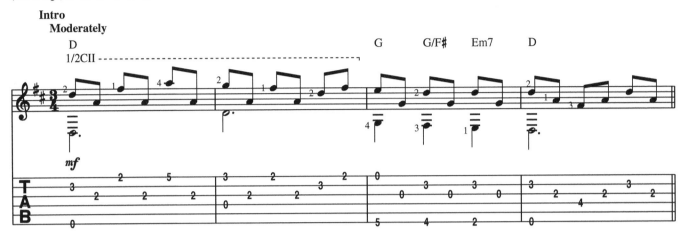

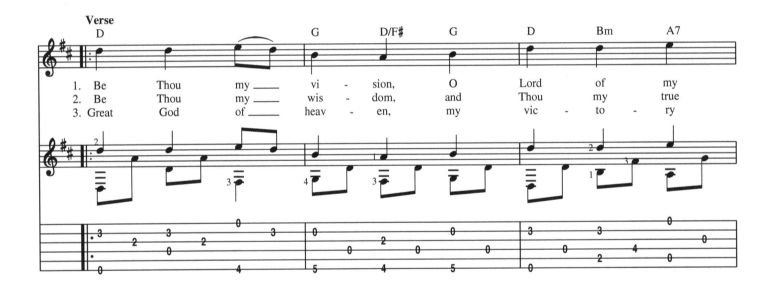

1. Be Thou my ____ vi - sion, O Lord of my
2. Be Thou my ____ wis - dom, and Thou my true
3. Great God of ____ heav - en, my vic - to - ry

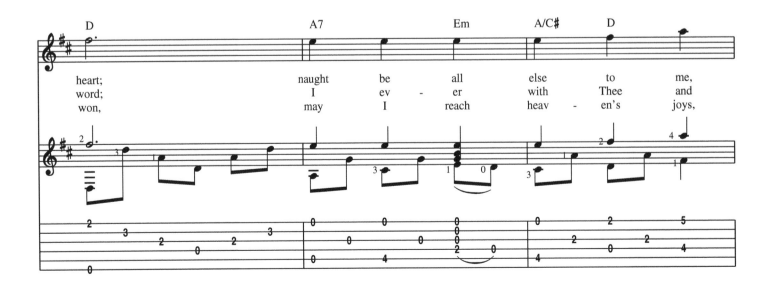

heart; naught be all else to me,
word; I ev - er with Thee and
won, may I reach heav - en's joys,

Blessed Assurance

Lyrics by Fanny J. Crosby

Music by Phoebe Palmer Knapp

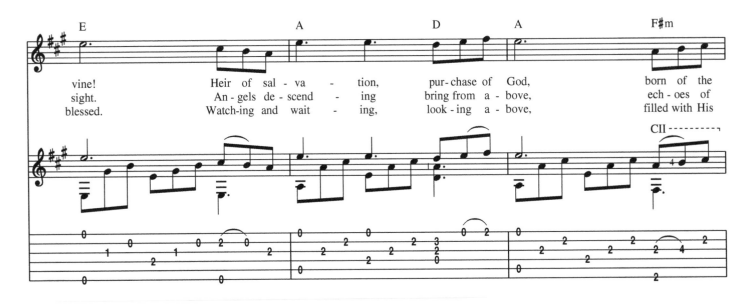

Christ the Lord Is Risen Today

Words by Charles Wesley

Music adapted from Lyra Davidica

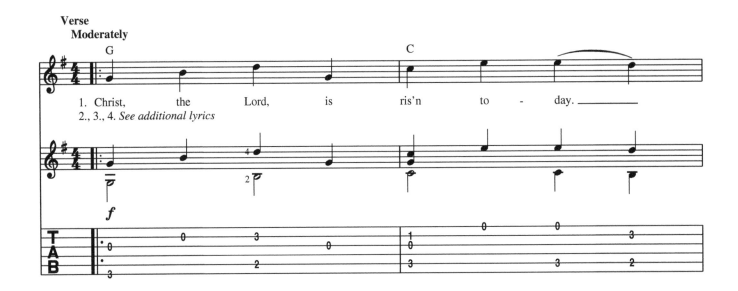

Verse
Moderately

1. Christ, the Lord, is ris'n to - day. _____
2., 3., 4. *See additional lyrics*

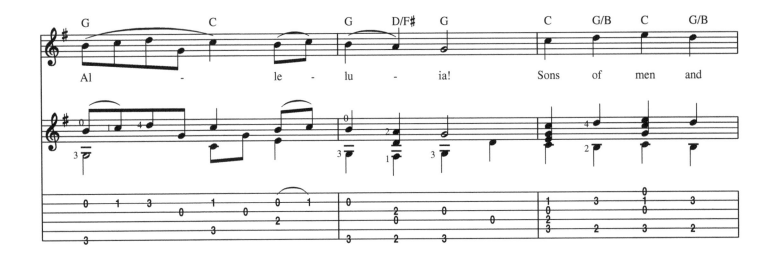

Al - le - lu - ia! Sons of men and

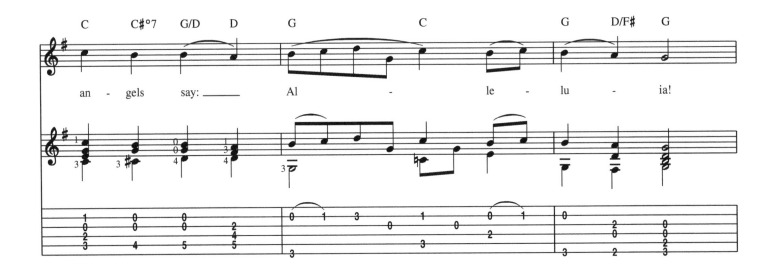

an - gels say: _____ Al - le - lu - ia!

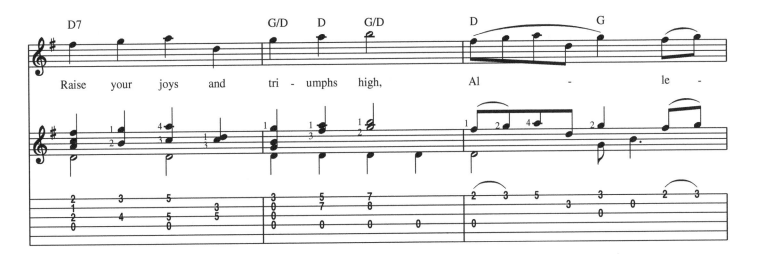

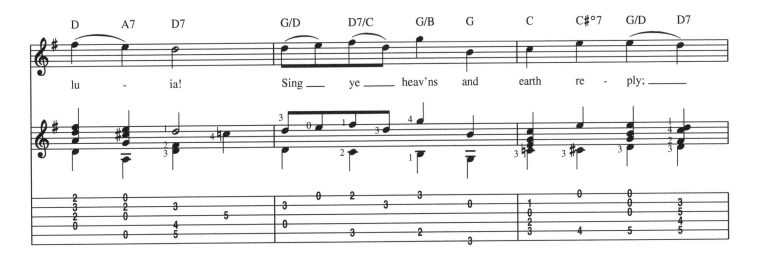

Additional Lyrics

2. Lives again our glorious King; Alleluia!
   Where, O death, is now thy sting? Alleluia!
   Dying once, He all doth save; Alleluia!
   Where thy victory, O grave? Alleluia!

3. Love's redeeming work is done; Alleluia!
   Fought the fight, the battle won; Alleluia!
   Death in vain forbids Him rise; Alleluia!
   Christ has opened Paradise. Alleluia!

4. Soar we now, where Christ has led; Alleluia!
   Foll'wing our exalted Head; Alleluia!
   Made like Him, like Him we rise; Alleluia!
   Ours the cross, the grave, the skies. Alleluia!

Come, Thou Fount of Every Blessing

Words by Robert Robinson
Music from John Wyeth's Repository of Sacred Music

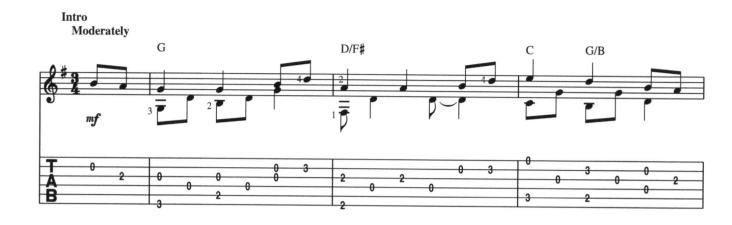

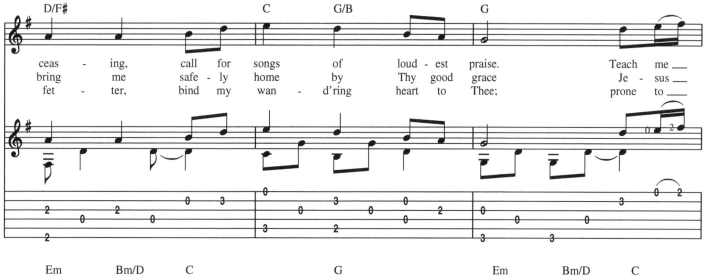

ceas - ing, call for songs of loud - est praise. Teach me ___
bring me safe - ly home by Thy good grace Je - sus ___
fet - ter, bind my wan - d'ring heart to Thee; prone to ___

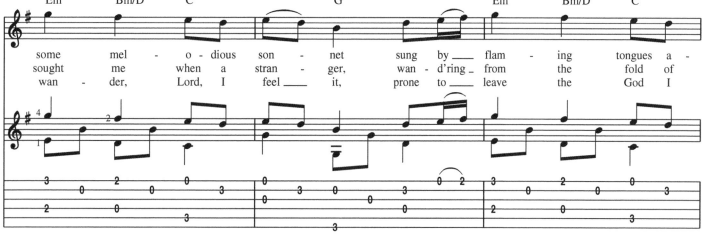

some mel - o - dious son - net sung by ___ flam - ing tongues a -
sought me when a stran - ger, wan - d'ring ___ from the fold of
wan - der, Lord, I feel ___ it, prone to ___ leave the God I

bove; praise His name; I'm fixed up - on it. Name of
God; He, to res - cue me from dan - ger, bought me
love; here's my heart, O take and seal it; seal it

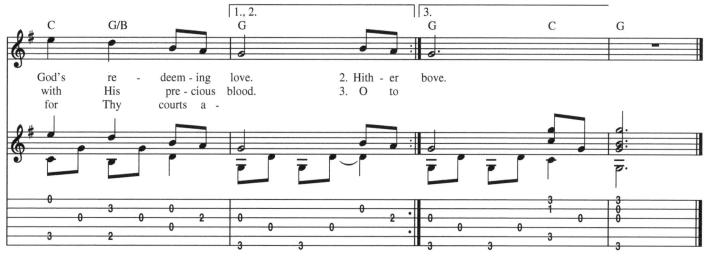

God's re - deem - ing love. 2. Hith - er bove.
with His pre - cious blood. 3. O to
for Thy courts a -

Fairest Lord Jesus

Words from Munster Gesangbuch
Verse 4 by Joseph A. Seiss
Music from Schlesische Volkslieder
Arranged by Richard Storrs Willis

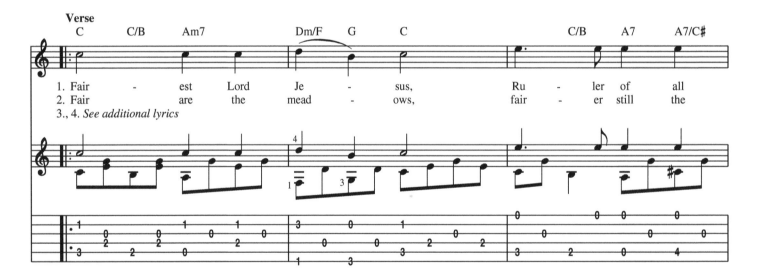

1. Fair - est Lord Je - sus, Ru - ler of all

2. Fair - are the mead - ows, fair - er still the

3., 4. See additional lyrics

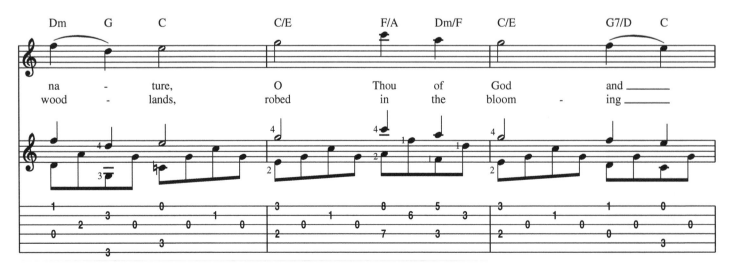

na - ture, O Thou of God and _____

wood - lands, robed in the bloom - ing _____

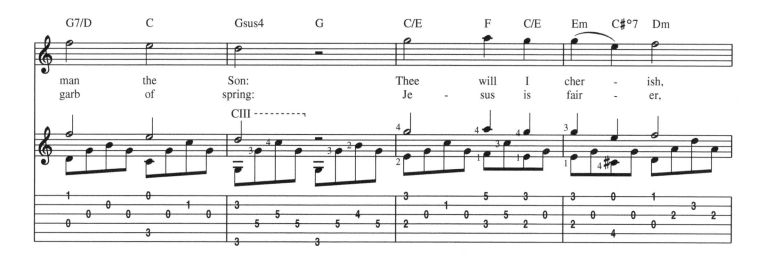

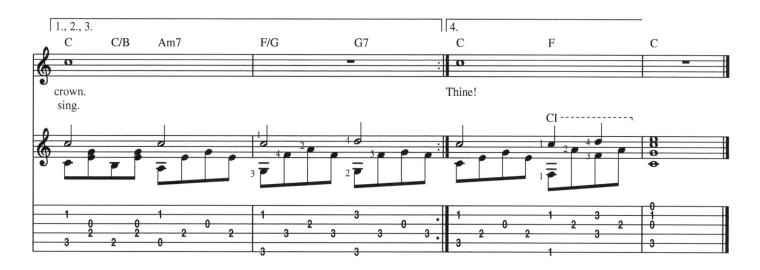

Additional Lyrics

3. Fair is the sunshine, fairer still the moonlight,
   And all the twinkling starry host:
   Jesus shines brighter, Jesus shines purer
   Than all the angels heav'n can boast.

4. Beautiful Savior! Lord of the nations!
   Son of God and Son of Man!
   Glory and honor, praise, adoration,
   Now and forevermore be Thine!

For the Beauty of the Earth

Words by Folliot S. Pierpoint

Music by Conrad Kocher

Drop D tuning:
(low to high) D - A - D - G - B - E

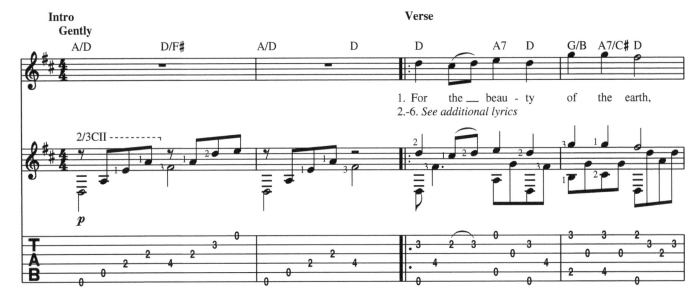

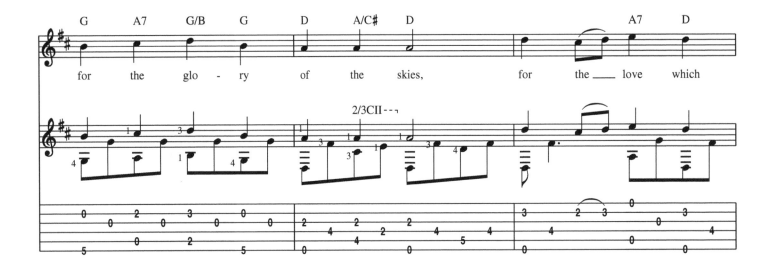

Additional Lyrics

2. For the beauty of each hour,
Of the day and of the night,
Hill and vale, and tree and flower,
Sun and moon, and stars of light:
Lord of all, to Thee we raise
This our hymn of grateful praise.

3. For the joy of ear and eye,
For the heart and mind's delight,
For the mystic harmony
Linking sense to sound and sight;
Christ, our God, to Thee we raise
This our sacrifice of praise.

4. For the joy of human love,
Brother, sister, parent, child,
Friends on earth and friends above,
For all gentle thoughts and mild;
Christ our God, to Thee we raise
This our sacrifice of praise.

5. For Thy church that evermore
Lifteth holy hands above,
Offering upon ev'ry shore,
Her pure sacrifice of love;
Christ, our God, to Thee we raise
This our sacrifice of praise.

6. For the joy of Gift Divine,
To the world so freely given,
For the great, great love of Thine,
Peace on earth and joy in heaven:
Christ our God, to Thee we raise
This our sacrifice of praise.

Holy, Holy, Holy

Text by Reginald Heber

Music by John B. Dykes

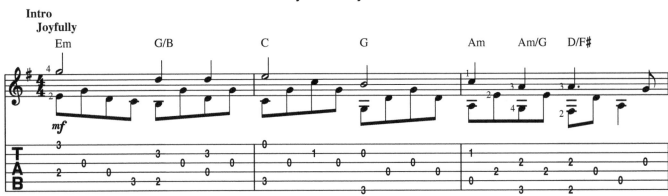

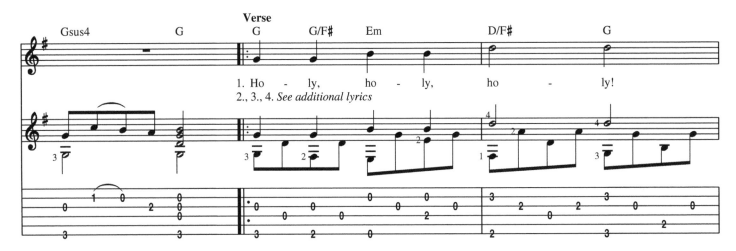

1. Ho - ly, ho - ly, ho - ly!

2., 3., 4. *See additional lyrics*

Lord   God   Al - might - y!   Ear - ly   in   the

morn - ing   our   songs   shall   rise   to   Thee.

Additional Lyrics

2. Holy, holy, holy!
   All the saints adore Thee,
   Casting down their golden crowns
   Around the glassy sea.
   Cherubim and seraphim
   Falling down before Thee,
   Which wert, and art,
   And evermore shall be.

3. Holy, holy, holy!
   Through the darkness hide Thee,
   Though the eye of sinful man
   Thy glory may not see.
   Only Thou art holy;
   There is none beside Thee,
   Perfect in power,
   In love and purity.

4. Holy, holy, holy!
   Lord God Almighty!
   All Thy works shall praise Thy name
   In earth and sky and sea.
   Holy, holy, holy!
   Merciful and mighty!
   God in three persons,
   Blessed Trinity.

How Firm a Foundation

Words by John Rippon's A Selection of Hymns
Early American Melody

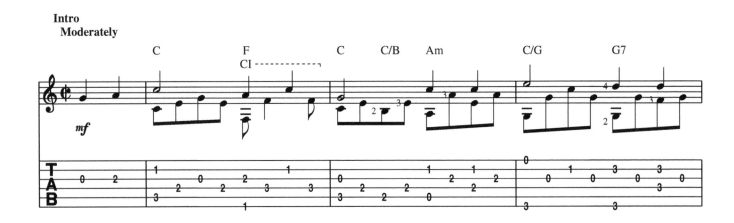

1. How ___ firm a foun- da- tion, ye saints of the
not, I am with thee, O be not dis -
through the deep wa- ters I call thee to

4., 5. See additional lyrics

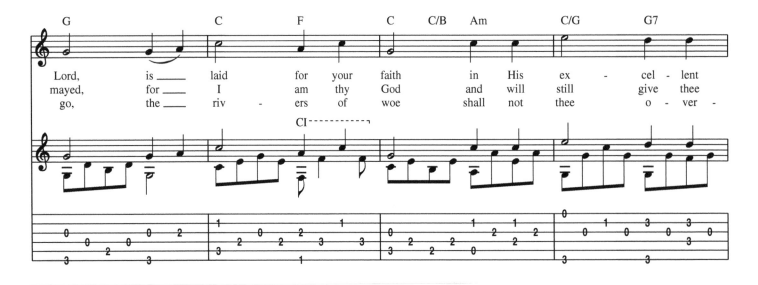

Lord, is ___ laid for your faith in His ex - cel - lent
mayed, for ___ I am thy God and will ex still give thee
go, the ___ riv- ers of woe shall not still thee o - ver -

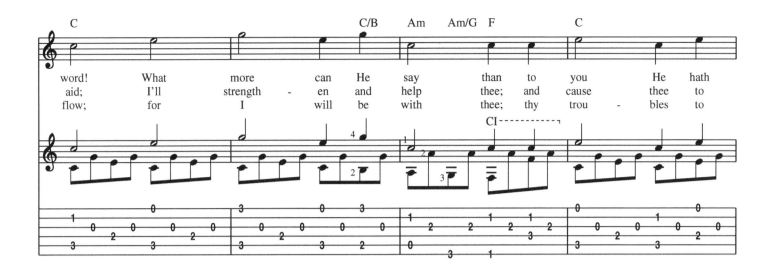

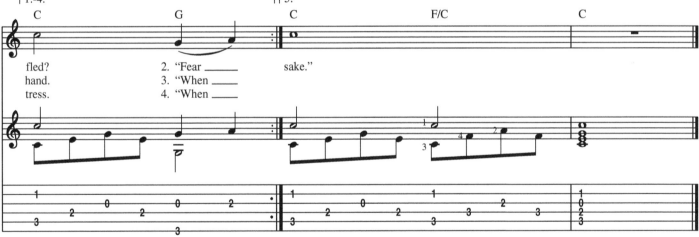

Additional Lyrics

4. When through fiery trials thy pathways shall lie,
   My grace, all-sufficient, shall be thy supply;
   The flame shall not hurt thee; I only design
   Thy dross to consume, and thy gold to refine.

5. "The soul that on Jesus still learns for repose,
   I will not, I will not desert to its foes;
   That soul, though all hell should endeavor to shake,
   I'll never, no, never, no, never forsake."

I Need Thee Every Hour

Words by Annie S. Hawks
Music by Robert Lowry

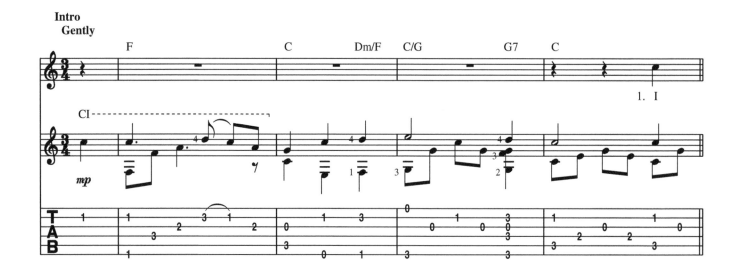

Chorus

need Thee, O I need Thee; ev - 'ry hour I need Thee! O

bless me now, my Sav - ior; I come _____ to Thee. 2. I
3. I

come _____ to Thee.

Additional Lyrics

4. I need Thee ev'ry hour;
   Teach me Thy will,
   And Thy rich promises
   In me fulfill.

5. I need Thee ev'ry hour,
   Most Holy One;
   O make me Thine indeed,
   Thou blessed Son.

In the Garden

Words and Music by C. Austin Miles

Drop D tuning:
(low to high) D - A - D - G - B - E

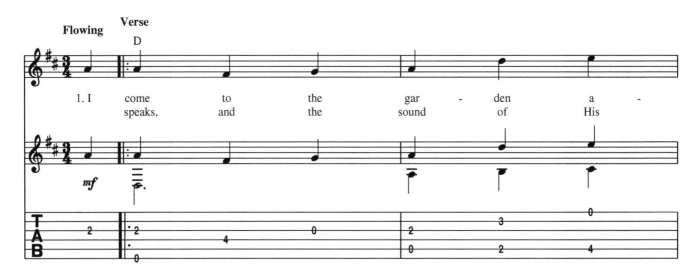

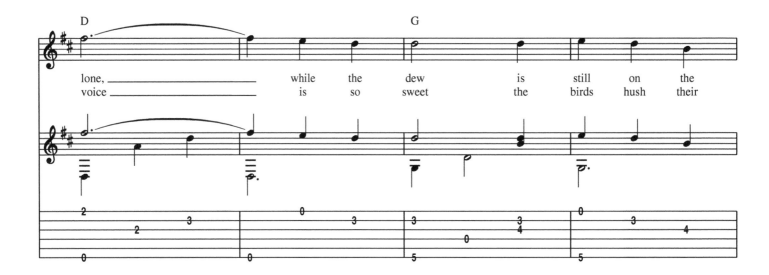

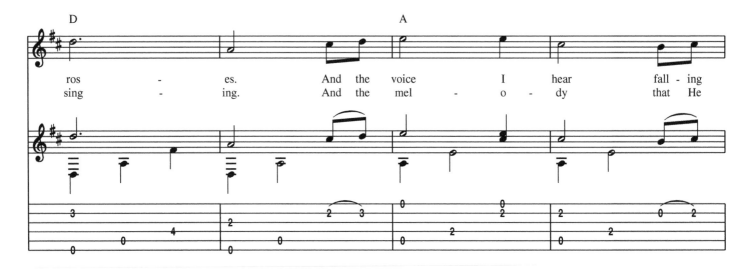

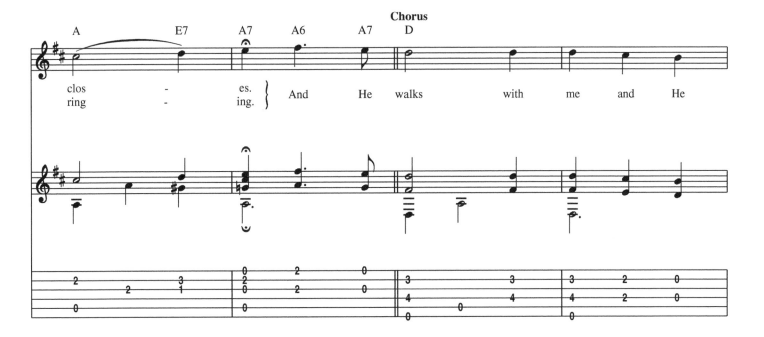

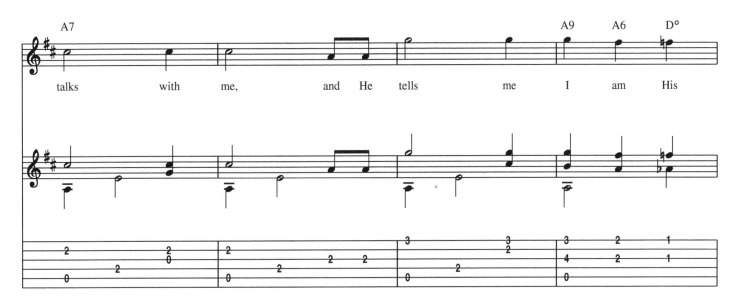

own. _____ And the joy we share as we

Bm　　D7/A　G　　　D/A　　A

tar - ry there, none oth - er has ev - er _____

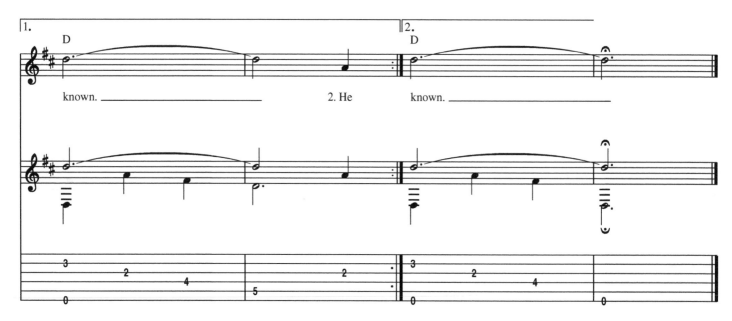

1.

D

known. _____ 2. He

2.

D

known. _____

Let Us Break Bread Together

Traditional Spiritual

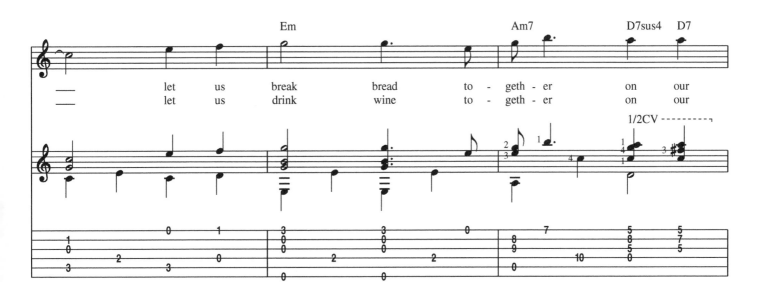

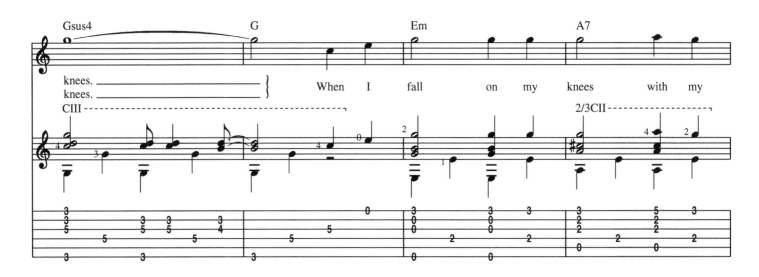

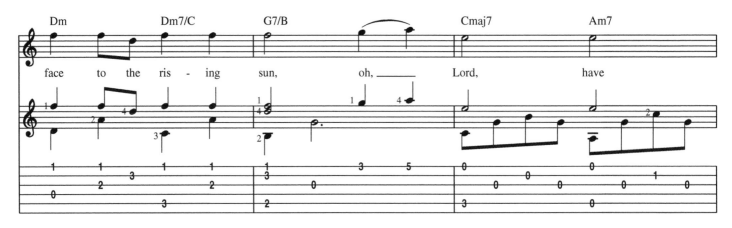

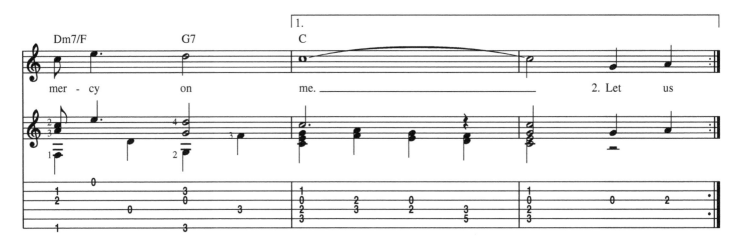

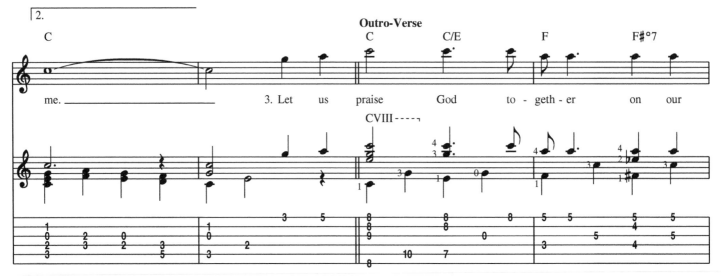

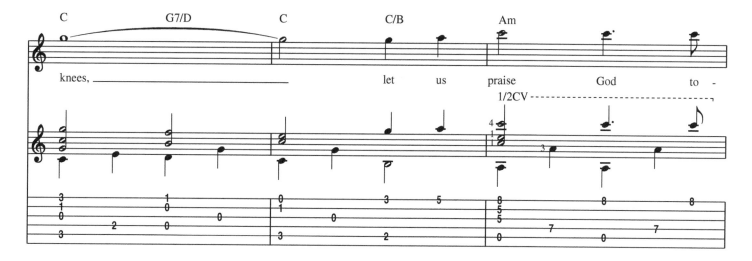

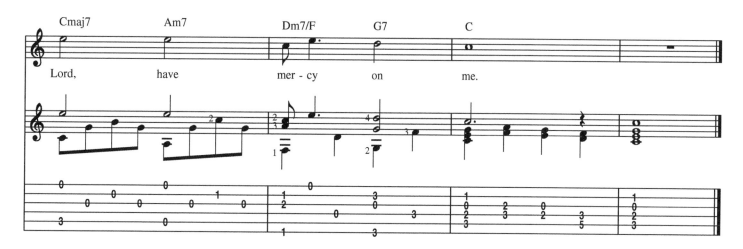

Joyful, Joyful, We Adore Thee

Words by Henry van Dyke
Music by Ludwig van Beethoven, melody from Ninth Symphony
Adapted by Edward Hodges

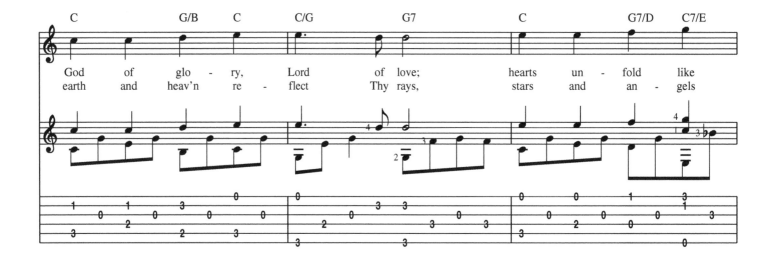

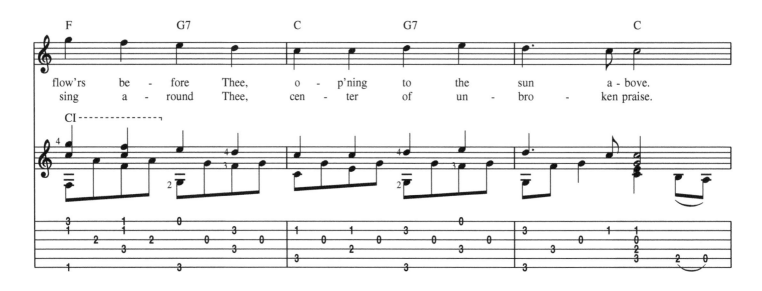

Additional Lyrics

3. Thou art giving and forgiving,
   Ever blessing, ever blest,
   Wellspring of the joy of living,
   Ocean depth of happy rest!
   Thou our Father, Christ our Brother;
   All who live in love are Thine.
   Teach us how to love each other,
   Lift us to the joy divine.

4. Mortals, join the happy chorus
   Which the morning stars began;
   Father love is reigning o'er us,
   Brother love binds man to man.
   Ever singing, march we onward,
   Victors in the midst of strife;
   Joyful music leads us sunward
   In the triumph song of life.

Just a Closer Walk With Thee

Traditional
Arranged by Kenneth Morris

Leaning on the Everlasting Arms

Words by Elisha A. Hoffman
Music by Anthony J. Schowalter

Drop D tuning:
(low to high) D - A - D - G - B - E

Verse
Moderately

1. What a fel - low - ship, what a joy di - vine,
2. *See additional lyrics*

lean - ing on the ev - er - last - ing arms; what a bless - ed-ness,

what a peace is mine, lean - ing on the ev - er - last - ing arms.

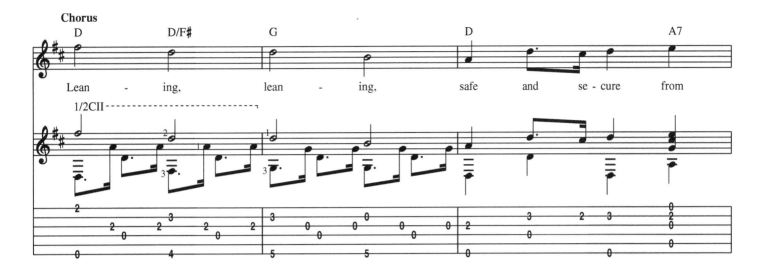

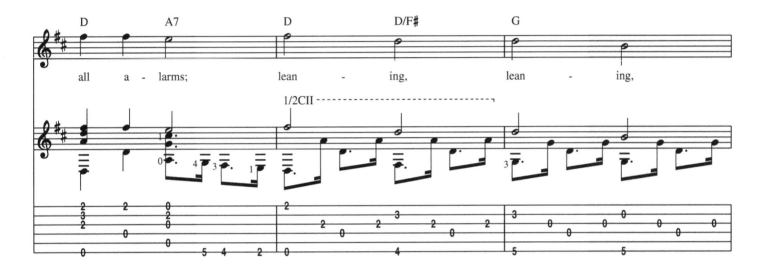

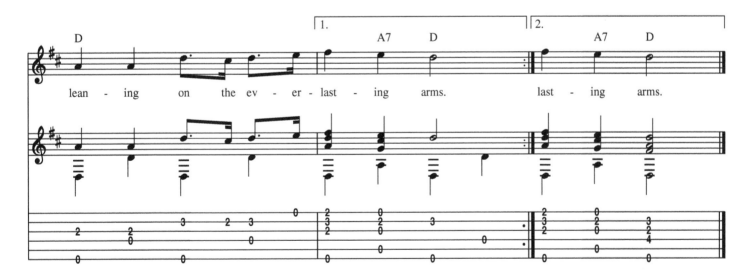

Additional Lyrics

2. Oh, how sweet to walk in this pilgrim way,
   Leaning on the everlasting arms;
   Oh, how bright the path grows from day to day,
   Leaning on the everlasting arms.

My Faith Looks Up to Thee

Words by Ray Palmer
Music by Lowell Mason

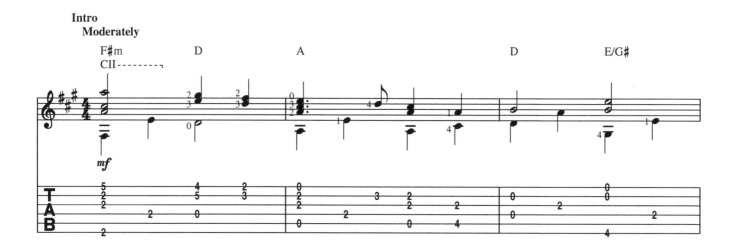

Verse

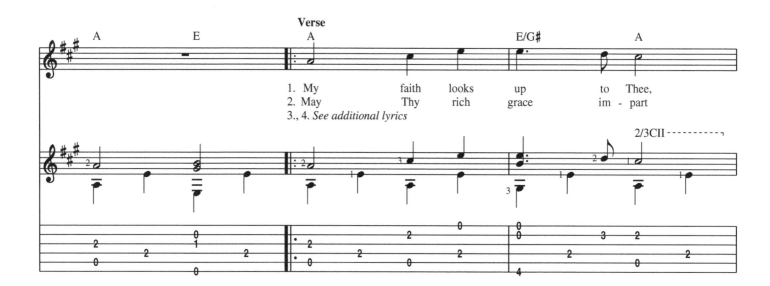

1. My faith looks up to Thee,
2. May Thy rich grace im - part
3., 4. *See additional lyrics*

Thou Lamb of Cal - va - ry, Sav - ior di -
strength to my faint - ing heart, my zeal in -

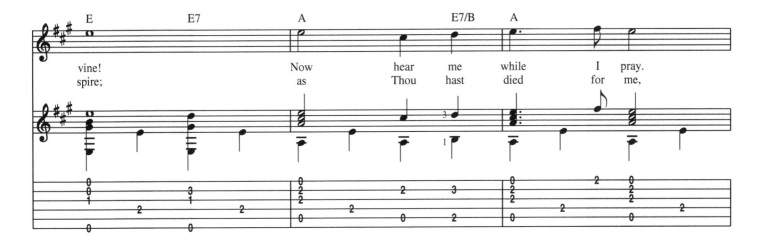

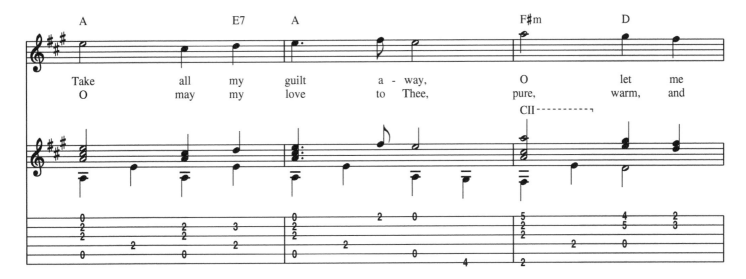

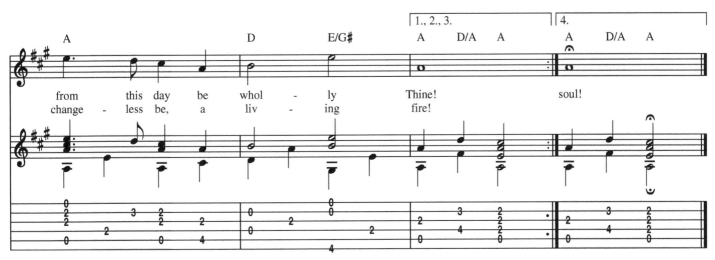

Additional Lyrics

3. While life's dark maze I tread
    And griefs around me spread,
    Be Thou my guide;
    Bid darkness turn to day,
    Wipe sorrow's tears away,
    Nor let me ever stray from Thee aside.

4. When ends life's passing dream,
    When death's cold, threat'ning stream
    Shall o'er me roll,
    Blest Savior, then, in love,
    Fear and distrust remove;
    O lift me safe above, a ransomed soul!

Nearer, My God, to Thee

Words by Sarah F. Adams
Based on Genesis 28:10-22
Music by Lowell Mason

Drop D tuning:

(low to high) D - A - D - G - B - E

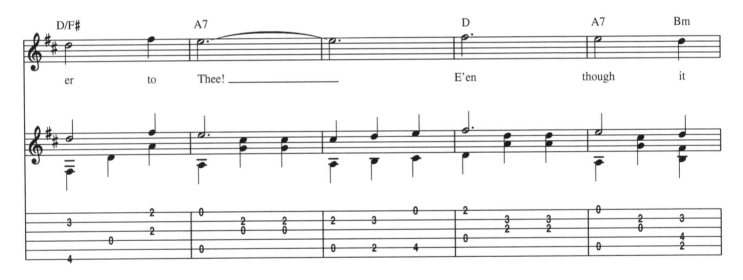

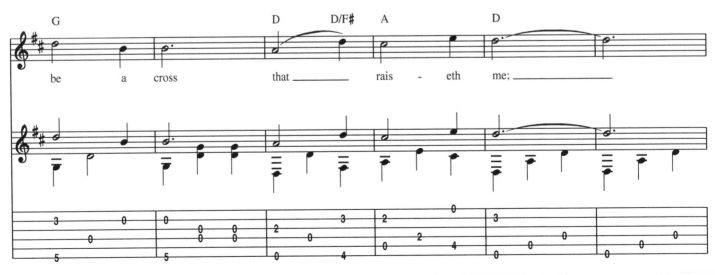

Additional Lyrics

2. Though like the wanderer, the sun gone down;
   Darkness be over me, my rest a stone.
   Yet in my dreams I'll be nearer, my God, to Thee,
   Nearer, my God, to Thee, nearer to Thee.

3. There let the way appear, steps unto heav'n;
   All that Thou sendest me in mercy giv'n.
   Angels to beckon me nearer, my God, to Thee,
   Nearer, my God, to Thee, nearer to Thee.

4. Then, with my waking thoughts bright with my praise.
   Out of my stony griefs, Bethel I'll raise.
   So by my woes to be nearer, my God, to Thee,
   Nearer, my God, to Thee, nearer to Thee.

5. Or if on joyful wing, cleaving the sky,
   Sun, moon, and stars forgot; upward I'll fly,
   Still all my songs shall be nearer, my God, to Thee.
   Nearer, my God, to Thee, nearer to Thee.

O for a Thousand Tongues to Sing

Words by Charles Wesley
Music by Carl G. Glaser
Arranged by Lowell Mason

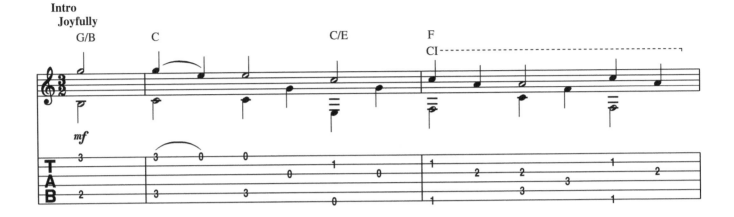

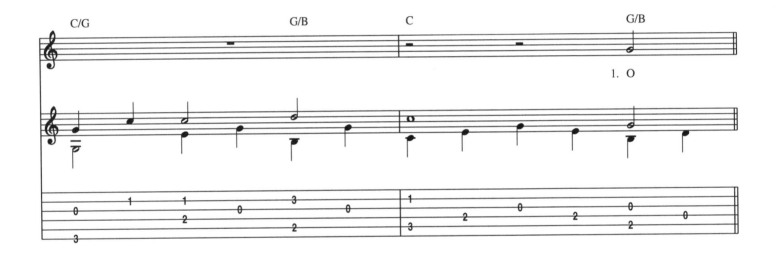

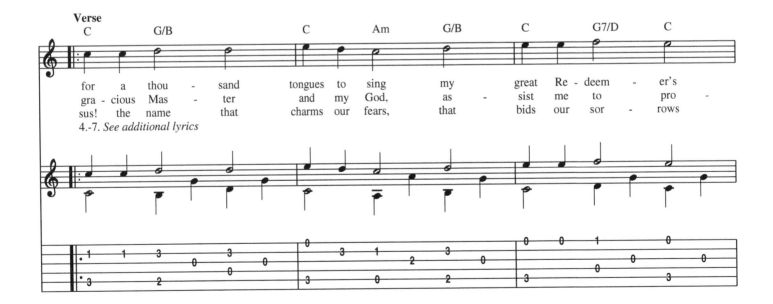

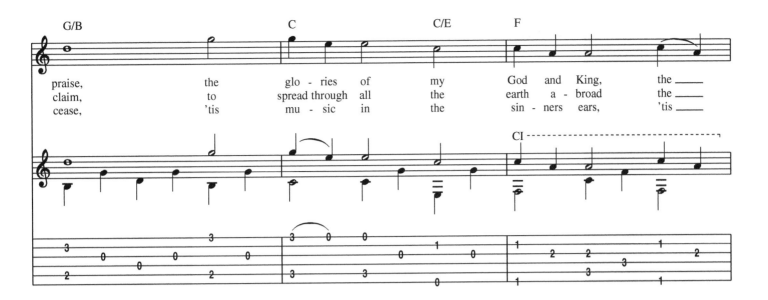

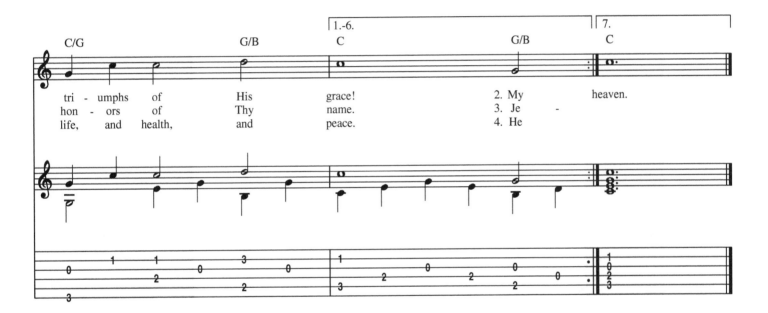

Additional Lyrics

4. He breaks the power of canceled sin,
   He sets the pris'ner free;
   His blood can make the foulest clean;
   His blood availed for me.

5. He speaks, and list'ning to His voice,
   New life the dead receive,
   The mournful, broken hearts rejoice,
   The humble poor believe.

6. Hear Him, ye deaf; His praise, ye dumb,
   Your loosened tongues employ;
   Ye blind, behold your Savior come,
   And leap, ye lame, for joy.

7. In Christ, your head, you then shall know,
   Shall feel your sins for giv'n;
   Anticipate your heaven below,
   And know that love is heaven.

O Master, Let Me Walk With Thee

Words by Washington Gladden
Music by H. Percy Smith

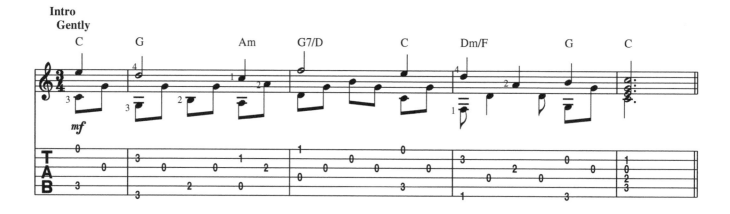

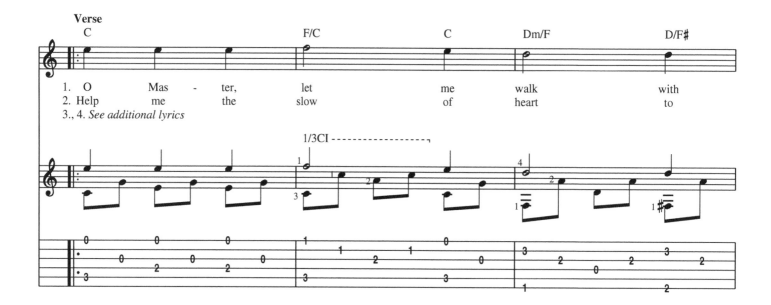

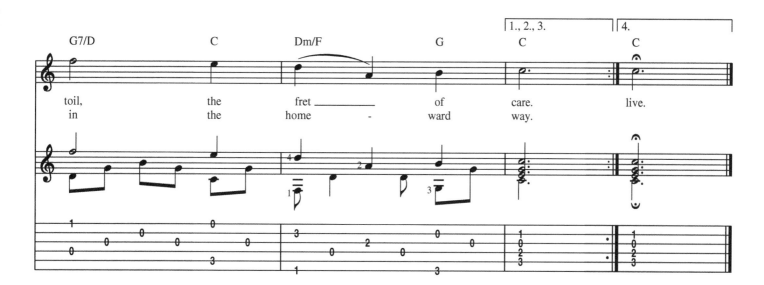

Additional Lyrics

3. Teach me Thy patience! Still with Thee
   In closer, dearer company,
   In work that keeps faith sweet and strong,
   In trust that triumphs over wrong.

4. In hope that sends a shining ray
   Far down the future's broad'ning way,
   In peace that only thou can'st give,
   With Thee, O Master, let me live.

O Worship the King

Words by Robert Grant
Music by William Croft

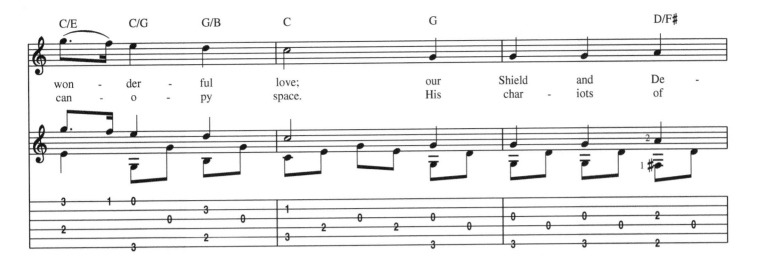

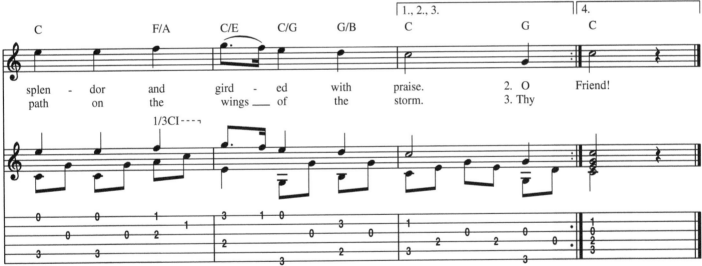

Additional Lyrics

3. Thy bountiful care, what tongue can recite?
   It breathes in the air, it shines in the light.
   It streams from the hills, it descends to the plain,
   And sweetly distills in the dew and the rain.

4. Frail children of dust, and feeble as frail,
   In Thee do we trust, nor find Thee to fail.
   Thy mercies how tender, how firm to the end!
   Our Maker, Defender, Redeemer and Friend!

Oh, How I Love Jesus

Words by Frederick Whitfield
Traditional American Melody

1. There

is a name ___ I love to hear, I love to sing ___ its
tells me of ___ a Sav - ior's love, who died to set ___ me

3., 4. *See additional lyrics*

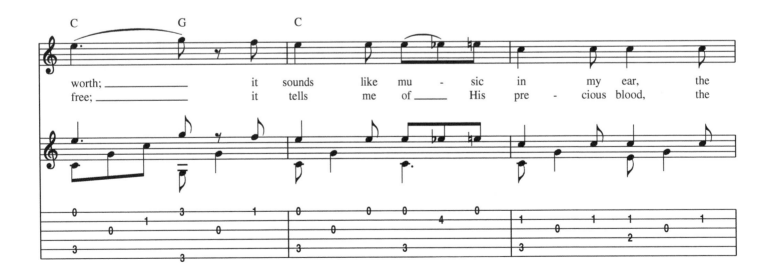

worth; _____ it sounds like mu - sic in my ear, the
free; _____ it tells me of ___ His pre - cious blood, the

Chorus

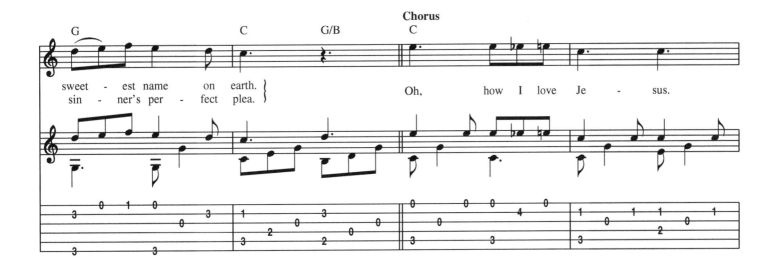

sweet - est name on earth. }
sin - ner's per - fect plea. }

Oh, how I love Je - sus.

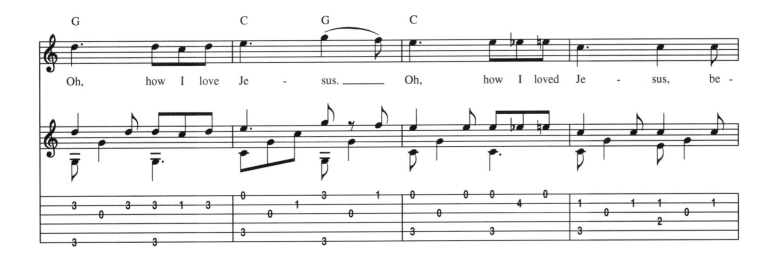

Oh, how I love Je - sus. ___ Oh, how I loved Je - sus, be -

cause ___ He first loved me.
2. It me.
3. It

Additional Lyrics

3. It tells me what my Father hath
In store for ev'ry day;
And though I tread a darksome path,
Yields sunshine all the way.

4. It tells of One whose loving heart
Can feel my deepest woe;
Who in each sorrow bears a part
That none can bear below.

Rock of Ages

Words by Augustus M. Toplady
V.1,2,4 altered by Thomas Cotterill
Music by Thomas Hastings

Drop D tuning:

(low to high) D - A - D - G - B - E

wound - ed side which flowed
save - ed and Thou a - lone.
be of sin the dou - ble
In of my hand the no price I

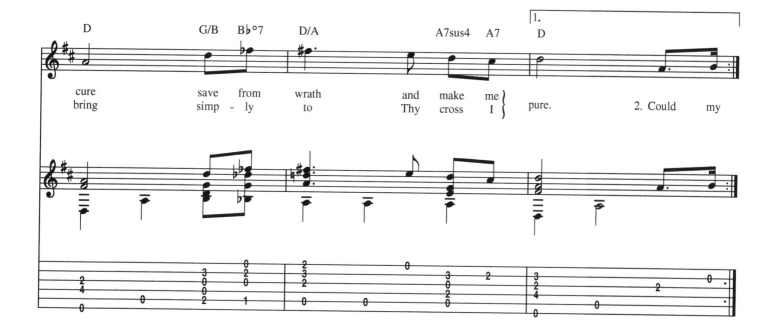

cure save from wrath and make me
bring simp - ly to Thy cross I } pure.
2. Could my

cling. Let me hide my - self in Thee. _____

Savior, Like a Shepherd Lead Us

Words from Hymns For The Young
Attributed to Dorothy A. Thrupp
Music by William B. Bradbury

Additional Lyrics

3. Thou hast promised to receive us,
Poor and sinful though we be;
Thou hast mercy to relieve us,
Grace to cleanse, and pow'r to free.
Blessed Jesus, Blessed Jesus,
Early let us turn to Thee;
Blessed Jesus, Blessed Jesus,
Early let us turn to Thee.

4. Early let us seek Thy favor,
Early let us do Thy will;
Blessed Lord and only Savior,
With Thy love our bosoms fill.
Blessed Jesus, Blessed Jesus,
Thou hast loved us, love us still;
Blessed Jesus, Blessed Jesus,
Thou hast loved us, love us still.

This Is My Father's World

Words by Maltbie Babcock
Music by Franklin L. Sheppard

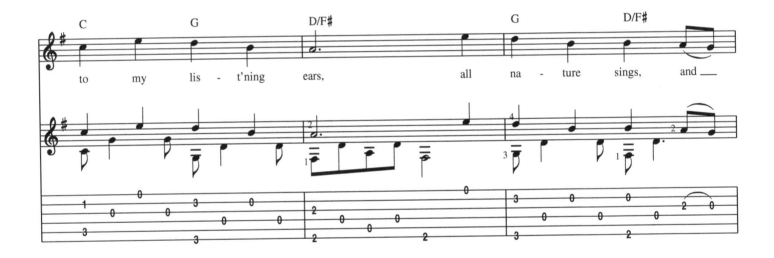

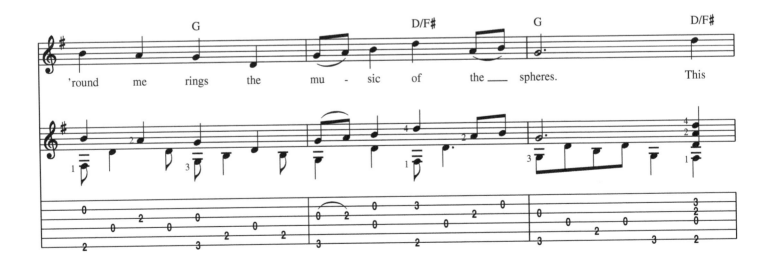

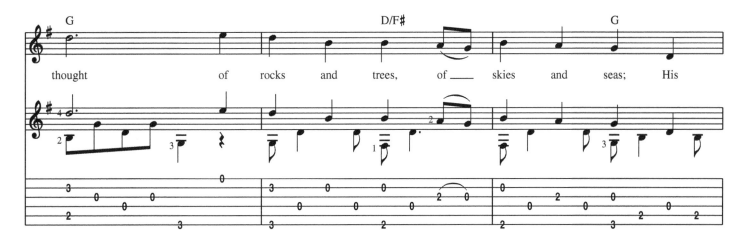

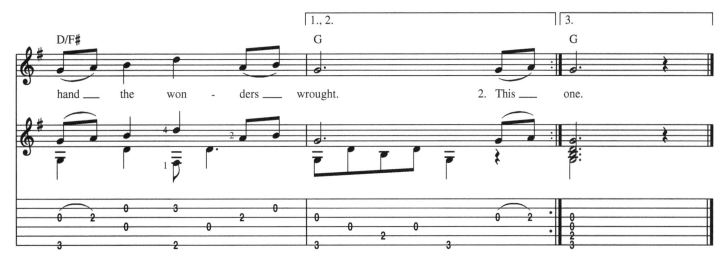

Additional Lyrics

2. This is my Father's world,
The birds their carols raise,
The morning light, the lily white,
Declare their maker's praise.
This is my Father's world,
He shines in all that's fair;
In the rustling grass I hear Him pass,
He speaks to me ev'rywhere.

3. This is my Father's world,
O let me ne'er forget
That though the wrong seems oft so strong.
God is the Ruler yet.
This is my Father's world,
The battle is not done;
Jesus who died shall be satisfied,
And earth and heav'n be one.

Were You There?

Traditional Spiritual

Harmony by Charles Winfred Douglas

Drop D tuning:
(low to high) D - A - D - G - B - E

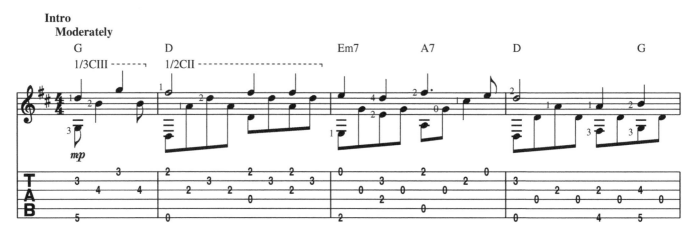

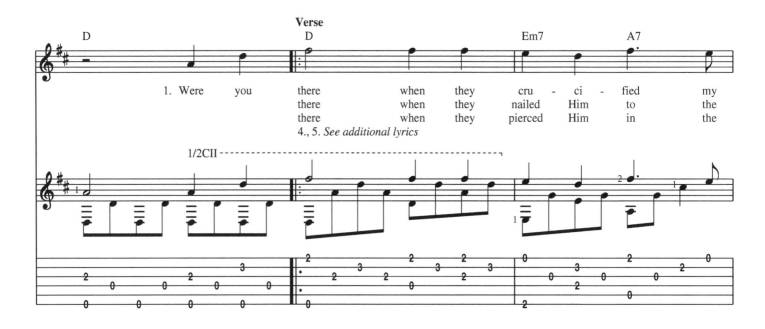

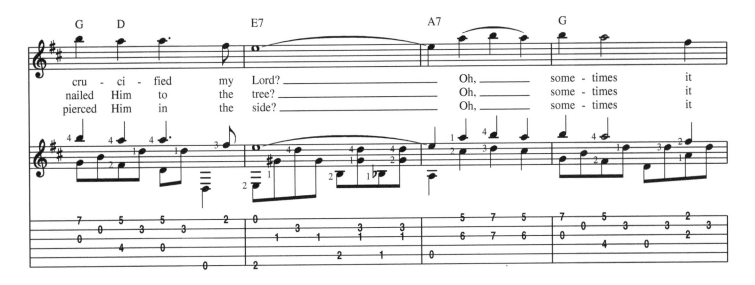

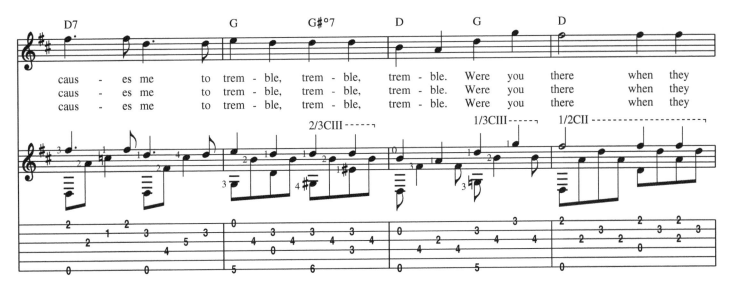

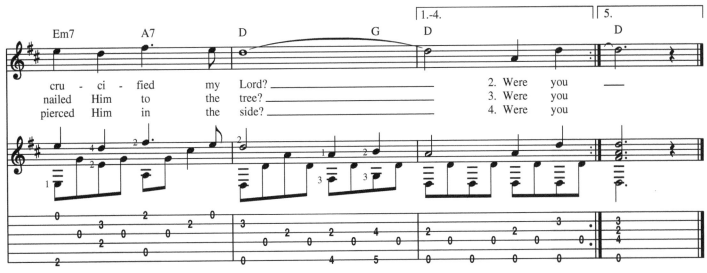

Additional Lyrics

4. Were you there when the sun refused to shine?
   Were you there when the sun refused to shine?
   Oh, sometimes it causes me to tremble, tremble, tremble.
   Were you there when the sun refused to shine?

5. Were you there when they laid Him in the tomb?
   Were you there when they laid Him in the tomb?
   Oh, sometimes it causes me to tremble, tremble, tremble.
   Were you there when they laid Him in the tomb?

What a Friend We Have in Jesus

Words by Joseph M. Scriven
Music by Charles C. Converse

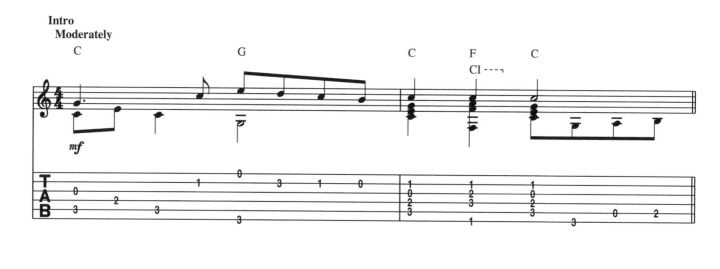

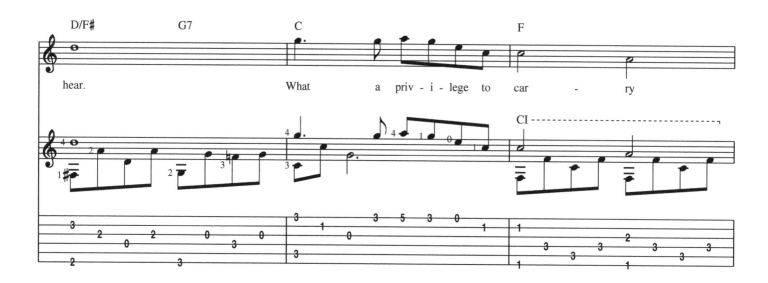

Additional Lyrics

2. Have we trials and temptations,
   Is there troubles anywhere?
   We should never be discouraged;
   Take it to the Lord in prayer.
   Can we find a friend so faithful
   Who will all our sorrows share?
   Jesus knows our ev'ry weakness;
   Take it to the Lord in prayer.

3. Are we weak and heavy laden,
   Cumbered with a load of care?
   Precious Savior still our refuge;
   Take it to the Lord in prayer.
   Do thy friends despise, forsake thee?
   Take it to the Lord in Prayer.
   In His arms He'll take and shield thee;
   Thou will find a solace there.

When I Survey the Wondrous Cross

Words by Isaac Watts
Music arranged by Lowell Mason
Based on Plainsong

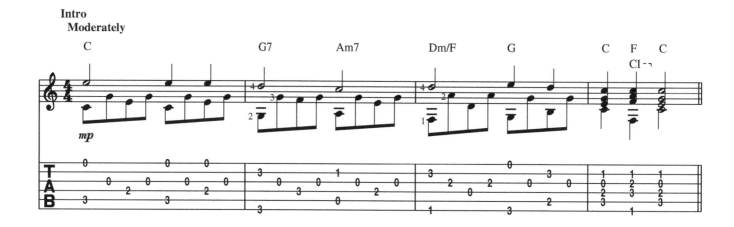

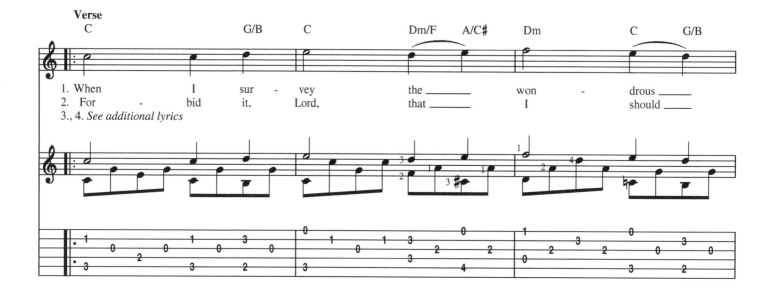

glo - ry _____ died.   My rich - est gain I _____
Christ, my _____ Lord.   All the vain things that _____

count but _____ loss   and pour con -
charm me _____ most   I sac - ri -

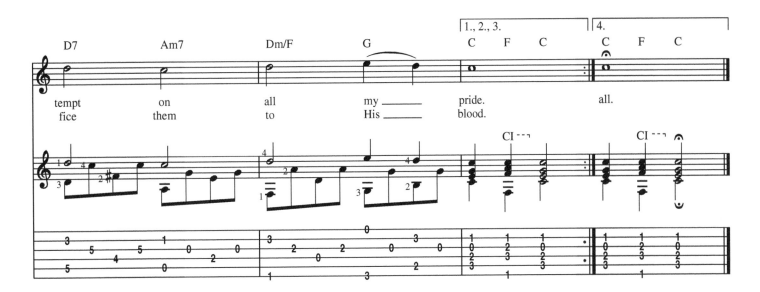

tempt on all my _____ pride.   all.
fice them to His _____ blood.

Additional Lyrics

3. See, from His head, His hands, His feet,
   Sorrow and love flow mingled down;
   Did e'er such love and sorrow meet
   Or thorns compose so rich a crown?

4. Were the whole realm of nature mine,
   That were a present far too small.
   Love so amazing, so divine,
   Demands my soul, my life, my all.

The Old Rugged Cross

Words and Music by Rev. George Bennard

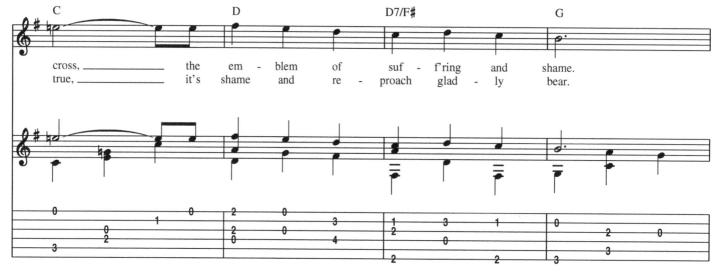

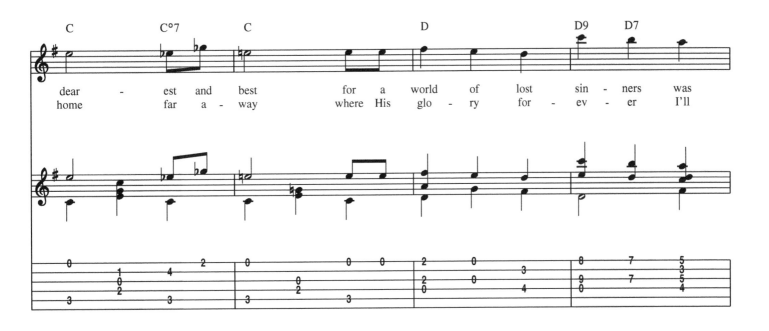

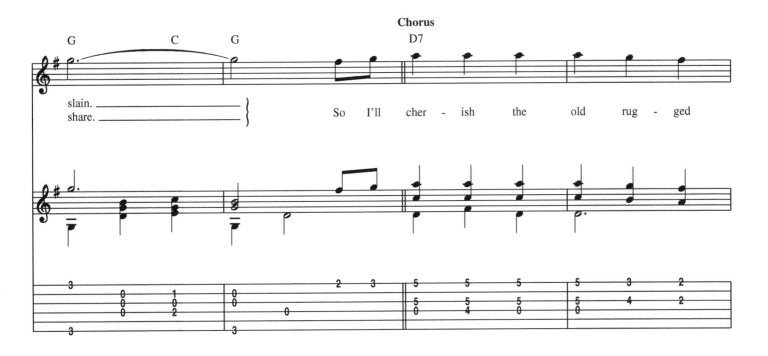

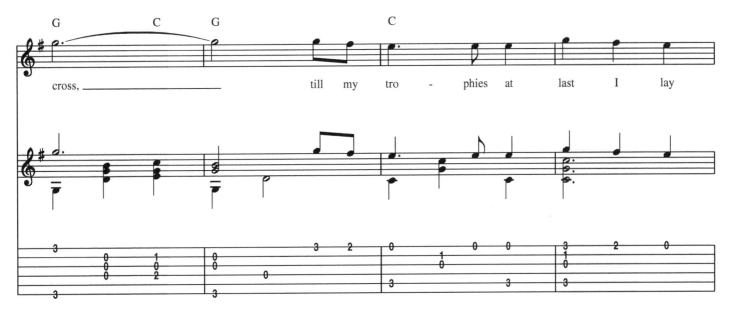

down. _____ I will cling to the old rug - ged

cross, _____ and ex - change it some - day for a

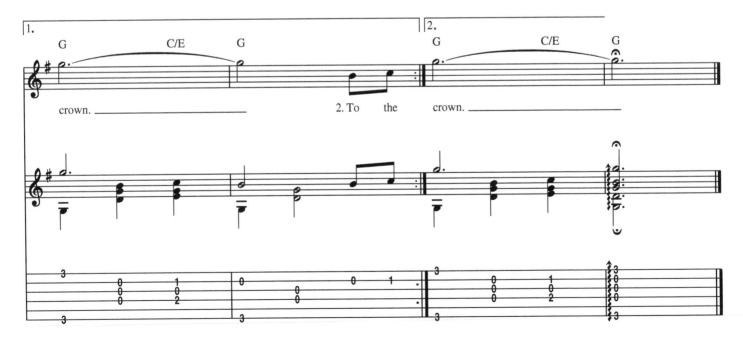

crown. _____   2. To the crown. _____